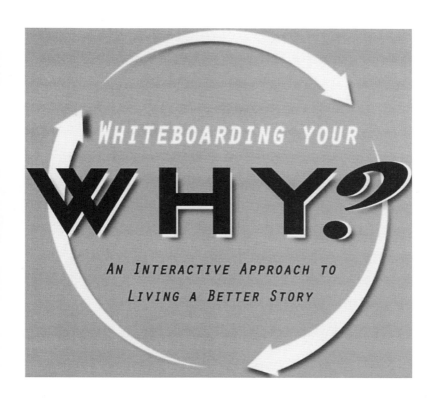

WHITEBOARDING YOUR

W H Y?

An Interactive Approach to Living a Better Story

RYAN AND TAMI CANADAY

Whiteboarding Your "Why?": An Interactive Approach To Living A Better Story

ISBN: 1548074713

ISBN-13: 978-1548074715

Published by Inspire Live Publishing

We dedicate this book to our three children:
Selah Rayne, Shiloh Eve, and Breck Brandon.

May you find your "Why?" and live the
best story possible . . . and always remember,
Mommy and Poppy are for you.

Special Thanks:
To Graham for his graphic artistry; you reminded us to keep
it simple. To our family and friends who allowed us the honor
to share some of their stories with you. To those who read and
re-read a manuscript of this book. To the St. Luke's United
Methodist Church community in Highlands Ranch, CO who
inspired us to keep leading others towards their "Why?".
And to everyone who has been for us and for this project!

CONTENTS

HOW WE GOT HERE

(Ryan) It is common for us to gather with friends in our living room or around our kitchen table to have some creative conversation about the ways in which we want to change the world. On this particular morning we got up early, brewed some Guatemalan coffee and grabbed the cinnamon rolls out of the oven [Tami makes a mean batch of homemade cinnamon rolls]. We had a friend visiting us from Key West for a couple of days. The three of us were sitting around the table that morning, talking about who we are, where we are going, our passions, and the kind of people we choose to be in the world, and "Why?". Our friend, Darren, has given his life to doing some incredible work with those in need of hope in Kenya, Zambia, and other African countries. For two decades, he has been involved in the work of empowering people from the margins, creating space for their voices to be heard, and helping them live better stories.

On this morning the conversation took an unintentional turn. We were no longer talking about his "work," we were talking about the "Why?" behind his work—why he had given himself to the project of standing in solidarity with some of the poorest communities on the other side of the world, why he cared, why he was passionate about this, about them, and why he was experiencing a renewed energy about this work.

"Why are you doing this work?" The conversation that emerged was full of enthusiasm. The energy was contagious! It was the first time he had articulated the "Why?" behind his work. And it had nothing to do with creating a mission statement, or getting the perfectly worded statement on paper in hopes of being more catchy, or getting more funding, or getting better grants. No. It had to do with all the things deep in the soul. It had to do with all the things, events, and people in his life that make him, him.

**It had to do with all the things that
brought him back to his story.**

And, he has a story. Darren knows what it's like to live on the margins, to lack a sense of belonging, and to have a plan in place to end his life. He knows what it's like to be barely hanging on by a thread, and he knows what it's like to be saved by glimmers of hope. Now he chooses to be a hope for other people, and for people who need it most. He chooses to inspire other people to be this hope for others. And the world needs more hope, right?

(Tami) When Darren was talking about the "Why?" behind his work, he came alive! You could see it. You could feel it. The "Why?" allows us to make the connections—to connect what we are doing with who we are. The "Why?" connects where we've come from to where we're headed.

**Without the "Why?", our work and our
movements are usually random.**

Our stories are our "Why?". We must know them, own them, remember them and share them; they are *our stories*. Many of us move about too quickly, jumping from one thing to the next, forgetting who we are, and forgetting all the reasons why we are doing what we are doing.

**Most of us are good at telling others "What?" we do,
many of us have never invested the time and energy
into figuring out "Why?" we do what we do.**

Life happens. So chances are, you have taken on a new role; started a new business, project, relationship, embarked on a journey of faith, recovery, forgiveness, healing, grief; or faced some other life-altering challenge, opportunity, or experience.

Why are you doing this thing? Why are you passionate about it? Why does it matter to you? Why are you willing to surrender in order to give yourself to this thing? When we figure these things out, the journey becomes so much richer, so much deeper, so much better.

This is an interactive approach that helps people articulate their [back]stories and find their "Why?". We present this material in various settings and offer a customized approach to individuals, groups, businesses, and organizations.

We have found this endeavor to be life changing— this project holds the power of changing the direction of one's life, one's path.

We have made some observations along the way. People have embraced their purpose and have begun living better stories. Consequently, we have created something simple and practical for everyone, and we are excited to share this creation with you. We have found the power in discovering our "Why?", and doing this together, with a small community of people. You are able to do it on your own. In our experience, the "Why?" becomes more obvious and discoverable when explored with other people. This book is an invitation for you to begin exploring your story.

(Ryan) You are able to begin exploring your story by whiteboarding. We have found whiteboarding to be an interactive and visual approach. It helps the creative process and is effective when connecting all the pieces that lead you to your "Why?". Whiteboarding allows your story, your dreams, and your passions to be bigger. It's visible—for you to see, for others to see. We're talking about vision here, and there is something about the communal act of whiteboarding that allows you to expand your vision. Too many people are limited by small dreams, a small vision, and a fear of giving themselves to something bigger. Don't be this person.

Life is too short. Life is too sacred.
Get a whiteboard. Get a vision.
And be all in when it comes to your life.

Step out of the box. Never think too literally here and let it be about the object; let it be about the process of living a better story. We have used various objects for whiteboarding: everything from a wall of plexiglass, a wall of paint that creates a whiteboard effect, a washer/dryer unit, cut up paper grocery bags [yeah . . . we were in a pinch], to an actual whiteboard on a stand or fixed to a wall. If you are joining a group to go through Whiteboarding Your "Why?", we encourage you to be creative. Have a large surface object available so you are able to capture critical messaging and movements for each participant. As a friend of ours often says, "The bigger the 'whiteboard', the bigger the vision."

Whether you are using this book in a group setting or on your own, this simplified, interactive approach incorporates the same visual storytelling into an illustrated process that all leads to a bigger picture of your "Why?"

"WHY?" THIS BOOK

*"Don't ask what the world needs. Ask what makes
you come alive and go do it. Because what the world
needs is people who have come alive."*
— *Howard Thurman*

(Tami) What we do becomes much more significant when
we understand why we are doing it. Most of us have never
fully engaged our "Why?". We have never moved beyond the
simplistic, not-really-wanting-to-go-deeper notion. Exploring
"Why?" is countercultural and difficult to articulate without deep exploration of our story. Knowing "Why?" never
has to be complex; it is simply the result of your story, your
experiences.

Have you ever felt stuck in a revolving, meaningless vortex?
Have you experienced cycling through the routine, feeling
drained and wondering if there is more to the story? Have you
settled for the status quo? It's time to unhinge, get unstuck,
move forward, and unlock the endless possibilities. It's your
story. Let's engage the deepest parts of you and move forward together. It's time to take your story somewhere, engage
the motion, and connect it to a place beyond yourself so that
you can discover your "Why?".

**Your "Why?" is at the core, the soul,
the heart of who you are.**

We are programmed to ask "What?" while often disregarding
"Why?". Intuitively we can ask and answer with *what* much
easier than asking or answering with *why*.

How often have you heard questions like this: What do you
do for a living? What are you passionate about? What do
you value? What are your priorities? What are your gifts?
Many of us have engaged in all or many of these questions

along our journey. How often do we miss some "ah-hah" moments by not asking "Why?" along the way. Think about your story. What in your story has had such a profound impact (we will refer to these impacts as "defining moments") that it intrinsically, at your deepest levels, allows you to be your true self? Who you are and what you do is essentially because of "Why?" you are and "Why?" you do.

**"What?" tends to keep us stuck. "Why?"
is the catalyst that gets us going.**

Instead of only asking the "What?" questions, challenge yourself to ask questions like: Why am I here? Why am I passionate about this? Why do I value this? Why is this a priority? Why is there energy here? Once you begin processing and engaging these questions differently, you will find a deeper purpose that drives you.

(Ryan) There is a YouTube video that recently went viral. This video separates "What?" and "Why?" so clearly. The comedian, Michael Jr., asks a Music Director in the audience to sing out a few bars of "Amazing Grace". This was an impromptu part of the comedic routine. The Music Director sang it beautifully, as you would expect. The catch? He was asked to sing "Amazing Grace" again, but this time he was prompted to imagine that his uncle just got out of jail, that he got shot in the back as a kid. . .

He sang it beautifully, he sang with soul, energy, power, and redemption! The crowd was in an uproar. His soulful sound commanded attention from everyone in the room. The second time, he knew what he was doing and more importantly, he knew "*Why?*" he was doing it.

This powerful video highlights the simple truth: What we do becomes much more significant when we understand "Why?" we are doing it.

You can check out the video here:
https://youtu.be/sfzpNVDzre0

This interactive approach helps you hold onto and embrace your story. You already know it. You have lived it. You have been there. We want to guide you to cultivate your authentic self so that you have a clear filter of what it means to live a better story in the world.

Here's the kicker: we are most alive when we expose our deepest vulnerabilities and insecurities. I know; that's counterintuitive, right? Culture tells us to be strong, to never show these things . . . and let the world see only our strengths. We are convinced that our weaknesses are our strengths. Weak is the new strong. Let's keep going.

It is our hope this newfound awareness brings much meaning, purpose, and fulfillment to your life.

May you experience the deepest kind of joy in
the journey of figuring out your "Why?", and may
you always find new life along the way.
– Ryan and Tami Canaday,
from our kitchen table, January 7, 2017

PART I: WHITEBOARDING YOUR "WHY?" OVERVIEW

"Instructions for living a life: Pay attention.
Be Astonished. Tell about it."
— Mary Oliver

"LIFE LINE"

(Ryan) When you know the overview of who you are and why you are here, your "Why?" becomes the thing that saves you—revealing and exposing that the story isn't over.

Your story is the thing that literally saves you.

Where do you come from? Where have you been? Being honest with your life and owning your story can be one of the most difficult—and most rewarding—things you can ever do. Honesty is a discipline. Think through the big movements of your story.

Spend some time in reflection. Look back on your story . . . even when it's painful and overwhelming. Take your time. It's not a race. Take an honest inventory of your story—your mistakes as well as the celebrations; your struggles as well as your accomplishments; your moments of failure as well as your moments of overcoming. Being honest with who you've been and where you've come from . . . this is the first step in the process of waking up.

Everyone has both positive and negative defining moments. As you reflect, remember these moments are the ones you experience in which you will never be the same; you are unable to change or reverse them.

(Tami) The moments that "define" you are entirely personal and dependent on your own interpretation. Only you truly know what makes you and breaks you. What events have happened that pull on your heartstrings? What events have happened that make you numb? What events have caused you to disconnect? What events made you feel most connected and aware?

When you start your Life Line, it will be from the beginning, as a child, to the present. When did you suddenly experience something profound enough in life where you were forever changed?

We will encourage you to identify up to 12 of these moments on your Life Line.

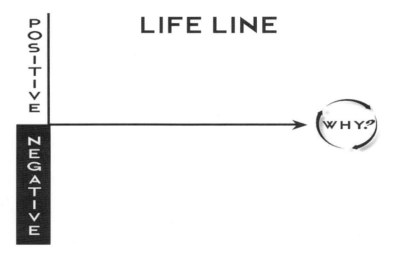

(Provided in Appendix B)

"DEFINING MOMENTS"

A positive defining moment may involve a job promotion, overcoming a fear, marriage, having kids, seeing a new perspective, finding transformation through humanitarian aid, making 'the team'. . .

A negative defining moment may involve failing, getting 'that diagnosis', a divorce, the loss of a loved one, the loss of an identity, being laid off. . .

A negative defining moment will always be precisely that, negative. What you do with these moments has the power to lead you to healing and to your "Why?". Moments of suffering and tragedy (negative moments) will never be positive. When we choose to find healing we must turn to redemptive aspects through our defining moments. Redemptive aspects provide us with a new lens which we utilize and depend on to react within the world.

These aspects move our story forward.

The redemptive aspects are limitless; they may often lead to a deeper understanding of compassion, realizing life's fragility, promoting a cause, standing alongside the broken, living with gratitude, or finding hope through healing.

"CIRCLE OF RUACH"
(Ryan) The ancient Hebrew people talked about wind, spirit, and breath as the life source—the creative energy that surges through all things, giving the universe its life and depth. They had a single word for this: *Ruach* [roo-akh]. Isn't that a fun word to say? Ruach! It's the thing that gives you and me life. We can't escape the presence of Ruach; it's the divine energy that is all around us, breathing life into us, always calling us towards the deepest things we know.

Throughout the book, you will use the Circle of Ruach to outline your story. *You will start by reflecting on your defining moments. Next, you will connect these moments with your deepest passions. Finally, you will engage how you live or want to live into your passions.* Each arrow in your story is interconnected, reminding you that your story is the thing that empowers you and moves you forward.

(Provided in Appendix D)

(Tami) Your Circle of Ruach will be a visual for getting to the core, your life source, and who you were created to be. You will be able to develop your "Why?" statement as the result. "Why?" you are is a result of where you have been and where you are headed. "Why?" helps make a clear statement of how your experiences have shaped you. "Why?" moves these experiences beyond yourself and out into the world. Your "Why?" keeps you intentional and allows you to live a better story.

"Because I . . ." helps you process your Life Line and Defining Moments into your final "Why?" statement.

First you will need to identify your Life Line (your story), including the positive and negative moments that make you, you. Your Life Line will act as the launching pad—leading you into your Circle of Ruach. Throughout each section, you will be invited to view our examples and then *Do The Work* [in the Appendix] as you begin to fully engage your "Why?".

Knowing your Life Line and how it fits into your Circle of Ruach will help you gain a clearer vision of your "Why?".

This interactive approach of whiteboarding your "Why?" will give you clarity to live with intention and worth as you find your own inspiration to infinitely impact lives beyond yourself.

May you get unstuck and move forward in knowing that you can live a better story!

PART II: "WHY?"
WAKING UP MATTERS

"Awake my soul. Awake my soul. . .
In these bodies we will live, in these bodies we will die
And where you invest your love, you invest your life."
– "Awake My Soul", Mumford & Sons

(Ryan)
The process of discovering your "Why?" is the process of waking up. Your soul is awakening to a greater sense of meaning in the world. This can be scary. This can be exciting. Your hands might start to get a bit sweaty, your heart might start beating faster, and the butterflies may be more active. Let's be honest; the process of waking up can often be a bit uncertain—you've been in a deep sleep, and now you're waking up and you have no idea exactly what you're getting yourself into.

When you discover your "Why?",
you are waking up to the newfound realities
of who you are and "Why?" you are here.

There's an old story told by Jewish rabbis. It's a story that has been passed down through the generations. It's a story about a first century rabbi.

On this particular day the rabbi was in a distant village gathering supplies. He noticed the sun was starting to set. It was getting darker. The rabbi quickly gathered his belongings and began making the journey back home. He made his way through the hills and alongside the stream, but by this time the sun had completely set. In the darkness and in his absent-mindedness, the rabbi took a wrong turn. Instead of arriving at the gates of his city, he arrived at the gates of a Roman fortress. Suddenly, a booming voice came piercing through the darkness: "Who are you, and why are you here?"

The rabbi stopped, looked up, and noticed the Roman guard standing atop the fortress. The voice sounded again: "Who are you, and why are you here?" Being a good, faithful rabbi, he answered the question with a question: "How much do they pay you to stand guard and ask those questions of all who approach?"

The guard, now seeing that this was not an intruder. It was a rabbi and he answered meekly, "Five drachmas per week, sir."

At that point the rabbi offered, "Young man, I will double your pay if you come with me, stand at my front door, and ask me those same questions each morning as I begin my day: 'Who are you, and why are you here?'"

Who are you?
"Why?" are you here?

(Tami) These questions matter. When you ask these questions, you experience a moment of awakening. Ask these questions often. Embrace the discomfort that comes in the asking. True engagement with these questions always leads to a fuller life.

Do you know who you are? Do you know why you're here? When it comes to your life, you are telling a story. You are the main character in your story. You get to determine what kind of story you are going to live.

You get to tell this story!

Ryan's story:
"I'm Ryan, I'm an alcoholic." These were the scariest words I ever uttered. The first time I said these words, I did so with fear and trembling. My voice was shaky. My hands were

clammy. I didn't know if I would say it when it came around to me. My head was swirling. All I could think about was: "I'm a pastor. What will people think about me now? I don't want to do this. I don't want to be here. How did I get here anyway . . . how'd it get this bad? It was never supposed to be like this." I said the words. I admitted it. And I felt lighter . . . a burden had been lifted in a way I never could have imagined.

No, recovery isn't that easy. Admitting my powerlessness and that life had become unmanageable, this was only the first step. There were 11 more steps, and the steps of a 12-step program involve real soul work. Coming face-to-face with my shadow side, dealing with my interiors [my character defects, my resentments, my self-centeredness], this is some of the hardest and scariest work I've ever journeyed through. But the rewards are great. I now know joy and peace and serenity, and I will go to great lengths to experience these things. I want to help other people experience them too. My battle with addiction is a piece of my story. I don't have to run from it. I don't have to hide it. I don't have to try to manipulate the negative moments to make them positive. No, there is nothing positive about choosing the bottle over my marriage or being told that my 18-month old daughter was begging for my attention but couldn't get it because I was passed out on the couch . . . again. There is nothing positive about planning the day around my next drink or forgetting where I hid the last bottle. And there is certainly nothing positive about puking through my nose and the hangover to follow.

**This darkness is a piece of my story,
and I must simply own it, speak it, and bring
meaning to it through reaching out to others
in the midst of their mess and brokenness.**

You see, in that moment of admitting who I was for the first time—in all the fear and unknowing—I knew what it was like to finally say "no" to shame.

Fear. Shame. Loss. Brokenness. These things mark my story. It is also in the midst of these things where I found and continue to find things like:

Hope
And healing
And redemption
And grace.

It's the deep paradoxical truth that so many people experience: We find hope only after first discovering the bottom.

When I was five years old, my parents divorced. It was an ugly divorce, and it stayed ugly for many years. Some of you have been there and you know exactly what I'm talking about. There were countless good and beautiful moments in my childhood. I had the privilege of growing up in home where I was deeply loved. My mom is still to this day one of my greatest heroes. But I also carried around a lot of fear . . . and fear ultimately turns into shame. I, like most adolescents, experienced failure. In 4th grade I was certain I was going to be an NBA player—the next Larry Bird. In 8th grade, I didn't make the team. I wasn't good enough. I didn't have much to offer academically either. During my Junior year in high school I took the ACT test. I'll never forget the day I received my test score. It was in the bottom 10 percent in the entire state of Missouri. I didn't want anyone to find out about this. It doesn't take much before we begin living into the narrative of: "I'm not good enough, and I don't want anyone to know that I'm not good enough." This kind of thinking does not lead to living a good story.

My brother was three years older than me, and from about the age of 16 he battled drug and alcohol addiction. I remember always being scared. I had nightmares of coming home and finding him dead. I hated visiting him in the county jail. I hated seeing him on the other side of that glass in that orange suit. There was something so embarrassing about it. Brandon brought a lot of suffering to our family. But he also brought a certain kind of joy . . . his bear hugs, his tenderness, his big heart, and his authentic spirit. He was easy to like, and lots of people liked being around him. He was a leader. He went to rehab and was sober for a few years. He relapsed. It was my first semester away in college, and I got the call from mom: "Ryan, you need to come home. Brandon has been killed in a car accident." He was 22 years old. Life would never be the same.

Everything I thought I knew about God and the world was turned upside down.

I was studying to be a pastor at the time. The truth is, I didn't trust God, and I didn't trust the people who were talking about God. Other people around me seemed to have things like joy, and peace, and serenity. I didn't feel cut for that stuff.

Tami's story:
I was hustling for worthiness, of feeling like I was 'enough', for a long time. Worthiness in my story was about reaching for an identity and affirmation in that which did not define me. My "Why?" and how I am uniquely wired is both innate and deeply rooted in how I have been conditioned to respond in the world.

I experienced loss of many loved ones at an early age. However, the loss of my dad has been the most defining. When I was 4 ½ years old my dad passed away from Leukemia. He was only 35 years old (Ironically, the same age as me writing this book today). I only have a handful of memories of dad, mostly pictures and stories I have been told. But through this I discovered the lens through which I began to see and interpret the world.

My "Why?" [and my lens] continued to evolve as death and its unsettling cycle continued . . . just before dad's death, my grandpa passed away from emphysema. Five years later my 18-year-old cousin died in a car accident, forcing the familiar feelings of life's fragility on me. I was left not knowing exactly what to do with these feelings. One month later, we lost my aunt to Lung Cancer, directly followed by the passing of my paternal grandfather another month later. When I was 12, I sat down with my school band teacher for a trumpet lesson. Nothing seemed abnormal that evening. However, at 7:00am the following morning that phone call came. Mom answered. I froze as *the look* presented itself on her face. She entered my room slowly. She sat down at the edge of my bed and shared the news: my teacher passed in his sleep from the flu.

I again found myself in this perplexing place where death was nothing more than provocative and scary. I was scared to admit that I wasn't strong. I was scared to process and listen to my feelings. I was scared that someone else close to me would die unexpectedly, without a moment's notice. My early perception of death left me confused, numb, and insecure.

I was deeply shaped by these experiences of loss. I would get close to people, only to release and pull away. I learned early that *life is fragile, life is delicate*. Because of this, it was difficult to allow myself full investment in any relationship. I also learned how to be guarded and skeptical of what each day would bring. Loss also taught me how to be sensitive, gracious, and loving, knowing each day that passes is nothing less than a beautiful gift.

My "Why?" emerged early. I knew who I was—my story, but I didn't know how to link that with my "Why?" For instance, why do I act and react in the world, often, within a framework of fear? Why fear? Because I acknowledge that when I am vulnerable and love deeply, it triggers the familiar fear of loss.

When I willingly decide to surrender and explore my own vulnerabilities, I can consciously decide to turn these feelings into gratitude and love.

I've learned that gratitude squelches fear.

I realize, and deeply respect, how much love, energy, and consistency my mom and grandma provided over the years despite their own losses. I respect my adoptive-dad [who I now call dad] for his gentle, unconditional love and for legally adopting me after marrying my mom when I was almost 11.

**Despite my losses, I have had
many constants in my life.**

The "constants" have taught me that I can embrace my "Why?" and lean into grace and empathy. The evolution of my Circle of Ruach has conditioned me to seek gratitude, hold on tightly, and love deeply without releasing, despite my fears.

May you find peace through allowing
yourself to be vulnerable.

Your Defining Moments Begin Your Circle of Ruach

**Defining moments are things
you cannot change or reverse.**

Do The Work

1. See examples in Appendix A. Complete your Life Line in Appendix B.
2. See examples in Appendix C. Identify your Defining Moments on your Circle of Ruach in Appendix D.

PART III. "WHY?"
YOU ARE WHO YOU ARE

"We have to address our emotional well-being . . .
The most common condition is not heart disease or diabetes
but it is isolation and social disconnection."
— Vivek Murthy, 19th Surgeon General
of the United States

(Tami) Ryan received a call from a couple in our community. Their daughter's life had just been taken due to a senseless act of violence. Ryan was asked to officiate the memorial service. This just so happened to be his first funeral as a pastor—and Brittany just so happened to be the age of Brandon (Ryan's Brother) when he was killed.

I remember it like it was yesterday. Ryan called me right before the service began, sobbing. He said "I don't know if I can do this . . . it's too hard, she was B's age. Her friends are here and they remind me so much of his friends. The same smells are even in the air." At some point during our conversation, he decided he was all in, and he would do the service. It might be raw. There might be tears. He might get choked up. It might not be a 'pretty service'.

But vulnerability is what makes these types of things come to life. And it's what brings people together and where we find some of our best connections.

It would have been easy for them to completely disconnect, withdraw, remain bitter, and do nothing. They lost a child. They lost a major piece of their identity. They lost Brittany. She was brutally murdered by a co-worker who was on work release and had an infatuation with her; the feelings had not been reciprocated. We never had the opportunity to meet

Brittany. We felt like we did from all the stories her parents have shared as we have journeyed with them through their grieving process.

Grief is an interesting thing. It can hold you captive. It also has the power to ignite a fire.

(Ryan) Grief can turn your world upside-down. It can make you question yourself. Grief can so easily persuade you to isolate and disconnect. It can also allow you to see and process the world differently, moving you in ways you never thought possible.

Brittany's parents continue to process this horrible tragedy in their own way. Bravely, they have sought places to share their story. Courageously, they continue to share and keep Brittany's story alive. They are finding connection through the grief and the chaos.

They aren't about to settle and sit comfortably in their pain and grief. They have been inspired to act. Brittany's death marks their story in a profound way and the healing process is exactly that . . . it's a process. Our friends know this: they don't want what happened to her to happen to someone else. They have become passionate about making a difference so that other families don't get that awful phone call that their child was murdered. They began collecting signatures for a petition to change the laws in hopes of preventing other tragedies like this.

(Tami) They have created a voice for Brittany. And they are moving their passion forward, allowing grief to fuel their passion and "Why?". They gathered over 12,000 signatures. Now they are hoping for a bill to be presented and passed on behalf of Brittany's story.

Allowing suffering to bring about real change in the world, this is one of the ways we redeem painful moments in our stories.

Her story is still being told; several years have passed since the funeral. We still consider Brittany's parents dear friends. They have stayed genuinely connected and willing to share their experiences. They have been highly involved in our projects and events through Project I Am For You. There will always be a genuine alliance and friendship between all of us.

Think about the Defining Moments you identified on your Circle of Ruach. As you reflect on these Defining Moments, the gravity of each event may feel different than it did when you experienced it. You may have been profoundly encouraged by these events. You may be deeply scarred by them. Or you may notice that what you thought was a Defining Moment wasn't actually as 'defining' as you originally believed when you were in the middle of it.

Reflecting on your story may lead you to see that you are more influenced by:

**How you process life events
than by the actual event.**

How has the residue of the event affected you? How have you processed the event? And, how has this event affected your circumstances, your happiness, and your story?

There is no prescription, no manual, no directions on how to navigate through chaos, transitions, addiction, illness, divorce, affairs, broken relationships, death of a loved one, new jobs, a diagnosis, being a new parent, being a grieving parent, caring for your parent—these events inevitably bring change, questions, and uncertainty in the unknown.

Ryan' Story:
"I wish I could preach on darkness every week . . . all year long." I recently made this comment to a colleague. She laughed. I think she thought I was joking. I was serious . . . for the most part. The truth is, I am drawn to darkness. Tami

likes to remind me how different our tastes are in movies and music. She says I gravitate towards the melancholy, and she's right. I am seldom bothered by darker films whose plots are left unresolved. These movies have the tendency to ask the best questions; they have a way of highlighting all the places within ourselves and the world that we've grown accustomed to ignoring. I prefer musical artists who are willing to go deep into their pain and suffering. The rawer the lyrics, the better. When they go to this place, I gain a better sense of my experiences of heartache and the heartache I see in the world. I know. This could all sound a bit creepy, right? However, when it comes to hope in the world, my starting places have become the darkest places.

> **These are the places where I tend**
> **to encounter the most beauty and**
> **experience God most deeply.**

During a recent interview, author and speaker, Brené Brown, was asked, after having lots of success as a writer and communicator: "Are you less afraid of the dark than you used to be?" Her response: "No. I'm not less afraid of the dark. I just know if you're willing to go in, there's beauty in it. But if you're not really afraid of the dark, it's not actually the dark."

It took me lots of years to get here, but I now embrace the dark. I'm willing to go in. Yes, it's still scary. Yes, I often go in with a bit of fear and trembling. Like Brené, I've experienced the beauty in there. When it comes to darkness, to the places of deepest pain in our lives, I am convinced: we cannot go around it or over it, we must go right through it. Head on.

> **We must go through the**
> **darkness to see the light.**

In my experience and observations, when we are willing to sit in that place, it is there we encounter hope. And the world is desperate for hope.

Pema Chödrön says: "Compassion is not the relationship between the wounded and the healed. Compassion is a relationship between equals. Only when we know our own darkness well can we be present with the darkness of others." I love this understanding of compassion! Simply put: that's what I want to be in the world.

Sure, I fail at this all the time. I'm a work in progress, and thank God the journey is about progress, not perfection. I want to be with others in their mess and brokenness. I want to do for them what so many others did for me: to stand with them, shoulder to shoulder, reminding them a new day is possible and despair might not have the final word.

That's what I'm passionate about. Being with people who have been overwhelmed by death, despair, and destruction. I'm drawn to them. They're my people. I want to play a role in the process of them experiencing God and beauty in the midst of their mess and brokenness.

On the days I do this, I am being most faithful to my path, my true-self, the one God created me to be.

Tami's Story:
How often have you been asked about what you love or what you are passionate about? For me, the answer was "Coffee" for years. Yes, I love coffee . . . I love everything about it. I love the details about where it is from, how geography affects the flavor profile, how the processing and altitude develops the distinguished quality and taste. I grew a deep respect and an appreciation for black coffee over time. It wasn't until I went through a "Coffee Master" program that I realized what drives me reaches beyond my love for coffee. My passion is the connection to the people, their stories, and why they do what they do—more than just the coffee.

It was easy for me to confuse what I was knowledgeable about with what I am passionate about. I had to dig a bit deeper and ask why. Getting to this point took many years and much reflection.

In early 2015 Ryan and I decided to celebrate our 10 year wedding anniversary by hosting a 2-day marriage retreat experience. We were convinced that our shared life experiences would inspire other couples to experience full life and depth in their relationship. And, we thought it would be a fun and challenging experiment to plan a 2-day event together.

I was afraid. I felt defeated before we even started the planning. As usual, I felt paralyzed by the fear and I didn't know how to move forward or even take the first step. I figured I would let Ry own most of the agenda, the platform, the talking and inspiring. I would take a step back because it was his identity, not mine. I felt his story was powerful, not mine. I know that fear makes me numb. Fear tells me to stay comfortable. Fear keeps me from moving beyond myself.

**When I am able to name my fears,
they actually begin to shatter.**

When the event began, I was honest. I was vulnerable. My heart was racing and I was extremely nervous. I was nauseous; being three months pregnant made it even more likely for me to throw up! But in the midst of fear, I shared how profoundly grateful I was for the opportunity. Ryan and I were in rhythm and we discovered synergy through planning and leading the experience together. The affirmation that I received that weekend began to wake me up to a new path.

When I surrender and explore my own vulnerabilities [especially fear, shame, and disconnection], these feelings have a strange way of turning into gratitude, love, and motion. After my third maternity leave, it finally made sense for me to surrender. And ironically, I quit my corporate job when Ryan was half way around the world, in Africa . . . can you even imagine that conversation? Yep . . . thank God for FaceTime.

This job owned me. It defined me. It consumed me. I worked for the same company for over 13 years. I settled without compromise. It took my identity. I gave every ounce of energy to my job. It sucked me dry. As much as I was present at work, I felt alone and isolated.

This job paid my way through college, it supported Ryan through his Master's Program, it provided for our children, and it offered great benefits. It was stable. But it was safe. I wanted to do something that gave me life, purpose, and rhythm. I couldn't forfeit all I had worked so hard for until I had identified my deepest passions (in correlation to my defining moments) and tangibly moved them into action.

Since the 2-day marriage experience and quitting my job, I have hosted various experiences on my own. I have stepped out in faith and trusted the process. I'm constantly taking steps to connect my passions with my authentic self, and it is liberating.

A sentence in Brené Brown's book *The Gifts of Imperfection* has stuck with me and helped me crawl out of the shadows of fear: "The dark does not destroy the light; it defines it. It's our fear of the dark that casts our joy into the shadows."

I have to remind myself to rise at the crossroads of fear; the cost is much more significant than the cost of failing.

I will rise in the face of fear.

You, too, are able to rise in the face of fear. It will be scary. There will be moments where you tell yourself: "I'm not made for this. I'll just go back to the old way." Resist this voice . . . turn off that noise!

Take that first step.

_____→

May you be empowered to figure out
who you are and "Why?" you are here.

"What?" Is A Result of Your Defining Moments.

Your defining moments often wire you beyond what is innate and move you into action.

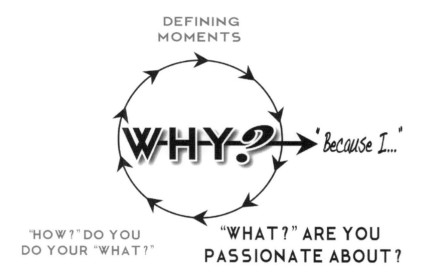

Do The Work

1. See examples in Appendix C. Identify "What?" Are You Passionate About [up to 6 things] in relation to your Defining Moments on your Circle of Ruach in Appendix D.

PART IV: "WHY?" FLOW IS BETTER THAN FORCE

*"When what brings you joy meets the need of
humanity is where you will find your calling."*
— Parker Palmer

(Tami) Our six year old daughter, Selah, has gained a very real appreciation for dance. She has no interest in tap dance, hip-hop, or the moves of modern dance. Her fondness of dance is solely for ballet. Perhaps she first fell in love with the tutus or the beauty of the dance itself. Selah tends to be graceful in her steps, twirling with discipline. Shiloh, our four-year-old daughter, moves differently in the world. Shiloh is high-energy, spontaneous, usually displaying exaggerated movements. Fascinating, isn't it? Their movement in the world reflects who they are in the world—their make-up, their wiring. There were many nights where Selah would dress up like a glittery ballerina and ask for the "Sugar Plum Fairy" to play over the blue tooth speaker, and she would tiptoe away, holding her hands in the appropriate ballerina position. After this went on for months, we finally signed Selah up for her first Ballet class. She was a natural. She loved it. Selah came alive in this moment.

This has everything to do with flow vs. force.

(Ryan) When you experience that natural kind of energy, the moments that make you come alive, the things that sustain you and keep you going, this is you finding your flow. Follow that energy. Give yourself to these moments, places, and things. These moments, places, and things give you purpose. They remind you who you are.

If you are currently giving yourself to the things that drain you, the things that make you feel like you're slowly dying inside, stop! These may be worthy endeavors and they are seldom your endeavors. These may be great and needed projects in the world, but they're not your projects. If you are always having to force these things, now is the time to let them go. Let them go and feel good about doing so. You've been called to a different path—walk that one, the one that brings you life, the one that reminds you who you are.

Flow is always better than force.

(Tami) Think about all the times you have found yourself in the space of flow vs. force. Have you paused long enough to accept why one thing comes natural and the other is an acquired skill? It is easy to get into the routine of our lives while seldom considering our story, our gifts . . . *who you are versus what you are.*

> We are *drawn* to our "Why?" because it is our natural, innate gift and produces energy.

> We are *driven* to our "Why?" because of the Defining Moments in our story.

Ryan's Story:
Do you remember the film, *Forrest Gump*? Much of the plot had to do with Forrest's [Tom Hanks] time in Vietnam during the war. In one of the more poignant scenes, Forrest enters and re-enters the combat zone to rescue his wounded comrades—literally picking them up, tossing them over his shoulders, and carrying them to a better place. He trudges through the mud and the thick brush to get to them, to be with them . . . he knows the way out. Forrest could have stayed where it was safe and comfortable, and he chose differently. He goes back in again. And again. And again. Forrest was clear about his story and how he wanted to live that story. He found his flow.

If I forget who I am and where I come from, or if I get caught up in trying to play the "humility card", I can quickly feel lost and lonely and disillusioned. You know about the "humility card" right? That's when we start saying things like: "who am I to go there?", or "what do I have to say to them?" That's not humility. That's fear and ego. The better question is: Why not go? Why not speak? The questions become: How am I living in integrity with my story? Am I living in alignment with who I am, where I come from, and where I want to head? Do you get the sense that Forrest Gump was walking the path to which he was called? I do.

Here's what I know: I experience profound joy when I own my story. When I own it, I am empowered to go through the mud and the thick brush, to go to the wounded and play a part in the healing work of the world. Healing isn't just about your healing; it's about you playing a bigger role in the work of healing in the world. When I own my story, I am empowered to go in, to be with those who are broken and wounded, and to journey together toward a better place . . . to help them experience God and beauty in the midst of mess and brokenness.

**Owning my story means that
I realize life is a holy, sacred gift.**

I cannot keep the gift unless I give the gift away. If I hold onto the gift as if it's all mine, then it's not really a gift; is it?

My work in the world has to be about this:

As a pastor.
A guide.
A leader.
A speaker.
A storyteller.
A volunteer in Africa.
A mentor in the Colorado State Prisons.

It's true. If we don't go out into the world and find a bit of suffering, then we might just become miserable. Real joy is found when we reach out to people in need, when we take the time to journey with them toward a better place.

When you engage in the art of sharing your story with others, your heart expands to see things you didn't see before, to sense things you've never felt. Lots of people are good at sharing their successes and celebrations. This is important. Celebrate well with others! But don't forget to share the pain, the times in life you didn't know how to take a step forward. The moments when everything was falling apart. Share this! This is one of the ways we redeem pain and suffering. Share your story. Don't hold back. The world needs it. You need it.

Healing is impossible without expansion of the heart.

There is not a more defeating feeling than loneliness. When my brother was killed in a car accident, I was certain that God had abandoned me and others. It was the most awful and indescribable feeling, and it lasted for months . . . even years. Until my early 20's, I had an understanding of God as the *deus ex machina* [god from the machine]. In some ancient Greek plays, there would literally be a machine to the side of the stage. When the plot would thicken towards adversity and defeat, the crane-like machine would drop the god-like character onto the stage. This character would simply fix the plot and resolve all the tension. My God was the deus ex machina, the god from the machine. When things got dicey, when the pain was unbearable, I expected God to drop in and fix it all. God didn't do this. The machine malfunctioned and failed. God was fake and phony and false, and I was quickly losing my faith in this god. In fact, this god died . . . thank God.

Years later, I came to know the God of life. It didn't happen overnight. It was a process, a long and painful process of struggling and letting go . . . old things dying and new things coming to life.

I no longer embrace the deus ex machina. God never steps in and out of our lives, relieving all the pain and tension, causing some to die while allowing others to live. It's way messier than this.

God is in all of it.

Where was God during the early morning hours of February 17, 2001? God was with Brandon as he took his final breath here on earth. God was the first one to cry. No, God was weeping—weeping with us and for us.

In your most painful moments, when the world cries out in agony, God screams back: "Me too! I've been there! I'm with you! You are not alone!"

When you speak your story, you are saying to others—who so desperately need to hear it—"Me too! I'm with you! You are not alone!"

**One of the most empowering feelings
is the feeling of knowing others are
for you, and they have your back—
that you are never alone.**

I have never felt more isolated and disconnected than I did the moment I walked into my first 12-step recovery meeting. It sucked. I thought I was unique. No one would understand my story, my problem, my shame, or my addiction. During that hour, almost everyone in the room shared. I thought it was a fluke. The first person shared. His story was freakishly similar to mine. The second story . . . hers was like mine too. And the third, the fourth, the fifth. We all had something in common: we were powerless over alcohol and our lives had become unmanageable. Thank God there was a way out, and many people in that room knew the way out and were willing to show me the way.

"Me too! You are not alone!" This message has been spoken so clearly in my story . . . spoken by God, spoken by others. When it comes to my story, there is a consistent thread of finding God and beauty in the midst of mess and brokenness. I want to help others share in this experience.

Tami's Story:
There is a great article, written by Pamela Druckerman, entitled "What You Learn in Your 40's". Whether you are middle-aged, in college, or retired, I think we all can all resonate with this statement:

"There are no grown-ups. We suspect this when we are younger, and can confirm it only once we are the ones writing books and attending parent-teacher conferences. Everyone is winging it, some just do it more confidently."

When it comes to your life, how often do you feel like you are winging it? As children, we believe that grown-ups have life all figured out with full affiliation and congruity between who they are, what they are, and why they are—and as we age, the truth is, it takes work to stay authentic to ourselves and our story. This is simply because we disconnect from our true self. We lose clarity. We lack energy. We force life. We lose purpose. We don't allow ourselves to discover who we were created to be in the world. I get it, I've been there.

**I like to call a period in my life
"My Two Years of No's".**

I was stuck in a cycle, a cycle of sorting out where I was going. The job I created transitioned to another state (without forewarning) so I was offered a promotion. The promotion ended up draining me, sucking every ounce of energy from me, causing disconnection from the things I cared about the most. My lack of happiness stemmed from my disconnection; it was a result of my personal skewed view of my purpose and self-worth.

I lost my zest. I lost my job that I loved and created. I lost my identity. I miscarried a baby. I was angry. I was resentful. I was bitter. I was ashamed of these "No's".

I knew my roots and what I was, but I struggled to find connection in who I was. I was unable to be fully vulnerable or express my shame and fear. I continued to wing it and cycle through the motions of life, waiting for my awakening.

**I wanted to "wake up" before I
even began cultivating my story.**

I wanted a "how-to" guide to point me in the direction of my purpose and my "Why?". I was longing for connection, joy, meaning, and wholeness. I was struggling, just like so many of you, because I was unable to identify or talk about the things that were in the way.

**Once I embraced my roots, it was actually quite
inspiring and simple to live into my "Why?".**

Once I decided to stay open and aware, it was grace that came along and woke me up. In voicing my shame and fear, I was able to break down barriers. I was able to embrace who I am and live with intention. It was grace that came along and showed me healing through redemption. Not the kind of redemption that comes along and casually makes everything pretty and magically all-good. It's the kind of redemption that allowed me to find meaning in the midst of fear, brokenness, and darkness.

Redeeming the loss of my [professional] identity has been a process. Finding worth in being a stay-at-home mompreneur is a process. Shifting my understanding of the roles I play has been challenging. I have had to realign my priorities and agenda in life. There will always be obstacles when finding new life; the unknown: the financial insecurities, the questions, the chance of failure. What I know is it's worth it and worth the risk.

I've always identified the passing of my dad as a Defining Moment since my childhood. Once I understood and processed the gravity of the loss, I realized that death itself wasn't ultimately what defined me, it was the absence [the loss] that held the power—the underlying fear that it created inside of me. The residue from the chaos and fear hijacked my worldview. The residue brought disorientation regarding my what ifs, my nevers.

I had to process the aspect of what could be potentially redemptive about dad's death. That redemptive aspect came as a deeper appreciation for the fragility of life and wired me to be a gracious, tender-hearted, and gentle peacemaker.

Let me be clear: "Redemption" doesn't come by way of putting a Band-Aid on a moment or an event.

**The redemption in my Defining Moments
became the deepest things I know, and it
is the way ["How?"] I live my life** . . .

As a Mompreneur.
As an Advocate and Life Coach.
As a Leadership and Project Coordinator in Africa.
As a Business Owner of Project I Am For You.

Loss in general has enabled me to realign my priorities of what the antidote to the fragility of life ultimately is: connection and "How?" I find connection.

Project I Am For You has evolved in correlation to my passions; I want others to find joy, wholeness, and to know someone has their back. I am leading various communities. I am working alongside and collaborating with multiple non-profits. I pursued life coaching and am *finally* finding purpose and synergy in life!

I am unable to forget my story and my experiences. I will consciously choose to allow my story to continue to refine me. Forgetting would forfeit who I am and why I am here. Forfeiting would keep me in the hasty cycle of unawareness and disconnection, and that is a vicious cycle. Forfeiting keeps me from discovering who God created me to be.

_____ →

May you embrace your story and stay aware of the people, places, and things that give you energy.

"How?" Moves Your "What?" Forward

"How?" is a result of who you are and knowing "What?" brings your passion to life.

Do The Work

1. See examples in Appendix C. Identify "How?" you do your "What?" [up to 6 things] in relation to your Defining Moments and "What?" Are You Passionate About on your Circle of Ruach in Appendix D.

CLOSING THOUGHTS

". . . What I can do is offer myself, wholehearted and
present, to walk with people through the fear and the mess.
That's all any of us can do. That's what we're here for."
– Shauna Niequist

(Ryan and Tami)
Your story leads to your "Why?". Your Circle of Ruach is the
catalyst to understanding how your Life Line and Defining
Moments lead to your "Why?". In identifying your "Why?"
statements, you are able to name who you are and where
you're going, but only from the heels of knowing where
you've been.

Your "Why?" is a filter.

It allows you to say 'yes' to all of the things that are congru-
ent with who you are. It allows you to run towards all of the
things that bring you and the world around you the deepest
kind of joy.

It allows you to say 'no' to all of the things that have nothing
to do with your story and what you are about in the world.
It allows you to say 'no' to everything that robs you and the
world around you of the fullest kind of life.

Because of this filter you can live a better story.

Ryan's Why Process:
Because I . . . know fear.
Because I . . . know shame.
Because I . . . know loss.
Because I . . . know brokenness.
Because I . . . know hope.

Because I . . . know healing.
Because I . . . know redemption
Because I . . . know grace.

Tami's Why Process:
Because I . . . know what it feels like to be afraid.
Because I . . . know gratitude shatters fear.
Because I . . . want others to know someone has their back.
Because I . . . have experienced the value and impact of a counselor.
Because I . . . want to create space for others to know they are enough.
Because I . . . have experienced unconditional love.
Because I . . . want others to know they can find peace in the chaos.

What is your process? What connections did you find between your Life Line and your Circle of Ruach?

Take some time and reflect on your journey.

You were created for this story.
You were made to live the fullest kind of life.
It's your time. It's your turn.
Get unstuck. Move forward.

We Are For You!

Do The Work

1) Consider your Circle of Ruach. See examples in Appendix E.
2) Start with "Because I . . ." and then formulate your final "Why?" statement in Appendix F.

APPENDIX A:
RYAN'S LIFE LINE [EXAMPLE]

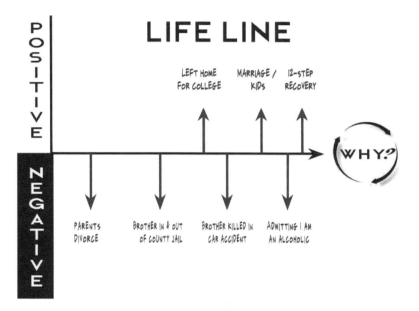

APPENDIX A:
TAMI'S LIFE LINE [EXAMPLE]

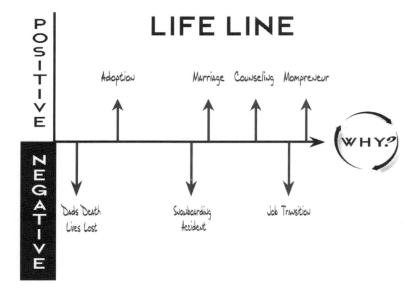

APPENDIX B:
YOUR LIFE LINE [DO THE WORK]

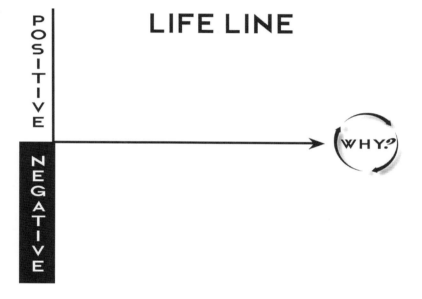

APPENDIX C:
RYAN'S CIRCLE OF RUACH
[EXAMPLE]

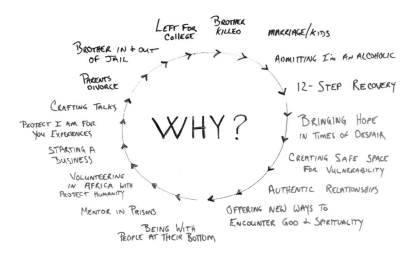

APPENDIX C:
TAMI'S CIRCLE OF RUACH
[EXAMPLE]

APPENDIX D:
YOUR CIRCLE OF RUACH
[DO THE WORK]

APPENDIX E:
RYAN'S "WHY?" [EXAMPLE]

APPENDIX E:
TAMI'S "WHY?" [EXAMPLE]

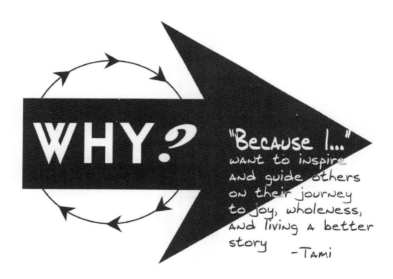

APPENDIX F:
YOUR "WHY?" [DO THE WORK]

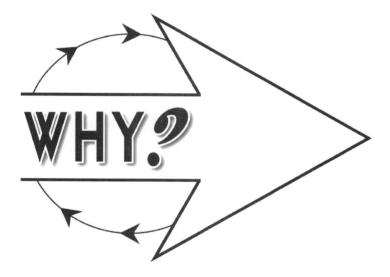

Whiteboarding Your "Why?" Facilitator Guide

Session 1: Whiteboarding Your "Why?" Overview
Provide an overview of *How We Got Here* and *Why This Book.*

- Facilitator(s): Share your Life Line of Defining Moments that have shaped, influenced, and created your story and identity (we recommend sharing your story in approximately 15 minutes or less).
- Facilitator(s) you set the atmosphere. Vulnerability creates empathy, connections, and trust. The participants will follow your lead.

Session 2: "Why?" Waking Up Matters
Defining Moments are categorized as moments that you cannot change or reverse.

- Participants: Take 30-60 minutes to develop your personal Life Line.
- Participants: Share your Life Line in approximately 15 minutes or less [up to 12 events] of Defining Moments that have shaped, influenced, and created your story and identity.

Session 3: "Why?" You Are Who You Are
Your Defining Moments often wire you beyond "What?" is innate [your passions] and move you into action.

- Facilitator(s): Share [up to 6 things] "What?" you are passionate about in connection to your Defining Moments.
- Participants: Identify and share [up to 6 things] "What?" you are passionate about in connection to your Defining Moments.

Session 4: "Why?" Flow Is Better Than Force
"How?" is a result of who you are and knowing what brings you life.

- Facilitator(s): Share [up to 6 ways] "How?" you do what you are passionate about.
- Participants: Identify and share [up to 6 ways] "How?" you do what you are passionate about.
- Ask the community to share "How?" they have seen you in action.

Session 5: "Why?" Statements (Create and Articulate)
Your Story Leads To Your "Why?"

- Facilitator(s): Share Your "Why?".
- Facilitator(s) and participants support each other, identifying each person's "Why?" statement.
- Begin with "Because I . . ."

ABOUT RYAN AND TAMI:

Ryan and Tami both are transplanted Midwesterners who met in college in Colorado. They decided to stay in the Denver area and were married in 2005. Ryan earned his Masters of Divinity in 2009 and currently serves as a Lead Pastor at St. Luke's United Methodist Church in Highlands Ranch, CO. Tami earned her BA in Psychology, then embarked on a successful 13-year business career. She recently left the corporate world, created Project I Am For You, and began living into her "Why?". Ryan and Tami now own Project I Am For You together; they are using their gifts, abilities, and heartbeats to inspire and transform the world. They live in Highlands Ranch, CO and have three children: Selah [6], Shiloh [4], and Breck [1].

– WEBSITE INFORMATION –

TO BOOK A KEYNOTE
LIFE COACHING
"WHY?" SESSIONS
PUBLIC SPEAKING COACHING
UPCOMING EVENTS
OUR BLOG

WWW.PROJECTIAMFORYOU.BIZ
WWW.WHITEBOARDINGYOURWHY.COM